RASPBERRY Pi 2

Advanced Tips and tricks

By Harry Colvin

Table of Contents

Introduction

Chapter 1- Definition

Chapter 2- Using the Raspberry Pi as a Router

Chapter 3- Setting up GPIO (General Purpose Input Output)

Adafruit Pi Code

Configuration of GPIO

Configuration of I2C

Kernel support Installation

Manual Installation of the Kernel support

Testing I2C

Chapter 4- Sensing movement

Configuring SPI

Chapter 5- MATLAB and Simulink for Raspberry

Setting up MATLAB and Simulink package

Configuration and testing

Starting the Support package Installer

MathWorks Account

How to use the MATLAB support package and the Raspberry Pi

How to use the Simulink support package and the Raspberry Pi

Chapter 6- Temperature Sensing

Hardware Layout

Configuration and Testing

Chapter 7- Email Notifier using LEDs

Remote SSH

Preparation of Python

Wire LEDs

The Python Script

Chapter 8- Printing

Conclusion

Disclaimer

While all attempts have been made to verify the information provided in this book, the author does assume any responsibility for errors, omissions, or contrary interpretations of the subject matter contained within. **The information provided in this book is for educational and entertainment purposes only. The reader is responsible for his or her own actions and the author does not accept any responsibilities for any liabilities or damages, real or perceived, resulting from the use of this information.**

Introduction

Raspberry Pi is a very useful device, and especially for the children who need to learn the basics of Computer science. This is why they need to know how to use the device..

Chapter 1- Definition

This book is a continuation of what we discussed in its first part, that is, Raspberry Pi 2. In this book, you learned more about the basics of Raspberry. You are now able to use SSH (Secure Shell) so as to access your Raspberry. You also learned the basics of how the Raspberry can be managed, including the addition and removal of users, as well as authenticating them by use of passwords. You are now able to connect your Raspberry to your PC, and also to perform the login process. The Raspberry can also be used as a file and media server. The device also supports the use of Bluetooth. Installation of this into the device was discussed.

The SD card of the Raspberry can be backed up and then restored whenever issues arise or whenever it is needed. Turning of the Raspberry into a Retro game console was also explored. The Bit Torrent Sync was also explored, so you should be able to work with it in Raspberry. The Tor server, which is common in the Raspberry was discussed in detail.

The above are the basics of the Raspberry which you should be familiar with before reading this book. This will make it easy for you to understand the content discussed in this book. In this book, we are going to discuss the more complex functionalities of the Raspberry. However, you need to know the basics of the device, so begin by reading the first part of the book if you have not already done so, and your work will be made easy.

Chapter 2- Using the Raspberry Pi as a Router

The Raspberry Pi can be used as a router. This will make it possible for you to use the network so as to access the Internet. However, you have to know how to set up the device as a router. This is what we are going to discuss in this chapter.

You need to begin by downloading and installing the Raspbian into your SD card. One can choose to use Debian. However, Raspbian is highly recommended for use, since it is highly optimized for the Raspberry. Installation of this into the Raspberry is very easy, so we will not explore this. If you are not familiar with it, there are many tutorials online which will guide you on how to do it, so consult them.

When you install the Raspbian images which are downloadable, you will find that the firmware for the Raspbian is an old version, which means that it cancause you some problems. In this case, it is recommended that you use *"Hexxeh"* which has been introduced recently. This can be easily be installed by use of the *"Hexxeh's rpi-updater."* However, before installing this, make sure that you have installed ca-certificates as follows:

```
sudo apt-get update && sudo apt-get install ca-certificates
```

Once the firmware has been installed, you need to activate it by rebooting the device.

The next step is to perform some configurations. In this case, we should begin by editing the file *"/etc/network/interfaces."* This can be opened as shown below:

```
sudo nano /etc/network/interfaces
```

Our aim is for the Internet facing IP to obtain an IP address via the SSH. The internal NIC should also have a static address. You need to use the subnet which you will use, so feel free to select the one of your choice. However, this should comply with RFC 1918. My file *"/etc/network/interfaces"* looks as follows:

 # interfaces(5) file used by ifup(8) and ifdown(8)

auto lo

iface lo inet loopback

#Onboard NIC to connect to the Internet

auto eth0

iface eth0 inet dhcp

#USB NIC to serve as internal gateway

auto eth1

iface eth1 inet static

address 192.168.160.1

netmask 255.255.255.0

network 192.168.160.0

broadcast 192.168.160.255

gateway 192.168.160.1

The above is the content of the file. In case you need to use a different subnet, just change the IP addresses given in the file so that it can fit your needs. Once you have made the changes, the file should be saved, and then networking should be restarted or the system rebooted as follows:

```
sudo /etc/init.d/networking restart
```

With the above command, the networking feature will be restarted and the changes will take effect.

The next step should involve the installation of the DHCP package server into the Pi. This will help in assigning addresses to our client devices. The installation can be done as follows:

```
sudo apt-get install isc-dhcp-server
```

We now need to edit our DHCP server configuration file. Open it by executing the following command:

```
sudo nano /etc/dhcp/dhcpd.conf
```

You will notice a lot of the comments in the file have been included. You can read them if you need for a better understanding. We need to make the server authoritative. The reason is because it is the only DHCP server we have in our Pi. At the top of the file, identify the authoritative line and then uncomment it. This is shown below:

 # If this DHCP server is the official DHCP server for the local
 # network, the authoritative directive should be uncommented.
authoritative;

To uncomment the line, you just have to remove the pound (#) sign which is before it as shown above.

The next step is to add a subnet to our file. You just have to scroll to the bottom of the file, and then add the following to it:

```
subnet 192.168.160.0 netmask 255.255.255.0 {
range 192.168.160.10 192.168.160.250;
option broadcast-address 192.168.160.255;
option routers 192.168.160.1;
default-lease-time 600;
max-lease-time 7200;
option domain-name "local";
option domain-name-servers 8.8.8.8, 8.8.4.4;
}
```

Note that in my case, I have used the subnet 192.168.50.0/24. If you need to use yours, then you have to change the addresses, which will be okay. The used servers in the above file are 8.8.8.8 and 8.8.4.4. These are Google public DNS servers. You might also want to use the DNS servers which your ISP provides. In this case, the IP addresses above should be changed so as to reflect this.

Once you have made the changes, save the file and then restart the DHCP service. This can be done as follows:

```
sudo /etc/init.d/isc-dhcp-server restart
```

Two ok messages, which are shown below should be received if everything ran correctly:

```
[ ok ] Stopping ISC DHCP server: dhcpd.
[ ok ] Starting ISC DHCP server: dhcpd.
```

In case you do not get these messages, then you have to repeat the process, and the problem will be solved. In case you get an error about no interface is in the proper address space, you have to double check the configurations and ensure that the static address used on eth1 is in the same subnet as the subnet for your DHCP. If you find that changes have to be made, do it and then restart the networking feature as we did previously.

You should now be in a position to plug your device into the eth1 (USB NIC) interface of the Pi device, and then obtain an IP address via the DHCP. Note that the furthest you can get in the network is your Pi. This is why we should enable the property IP forwarding on the device so as to solve the problem.

To do this, begin by running the following command:

```
sudo echo 1 > /proc/sys/net/ipv4/ip_forward
```

In the next step, we need to edit the file *"/etc/sysctl.conf."* Uncomment the line which says *"net.ipv4.ip_forward = 1"* as shown below:

Begin by opening the file as follows:

```
sudo nano /etc/sysctl.conf
```

The uncommenting should be done as follows:

Uncomment the next line to enable packet forwarding for IPv4

net.ipv4.ip_forward=1

Note that we have removed the pound (#) sign from the line as shown above, so do it in your system. You then have to save the file and its changes.

We now need to allow NAT (Network Address Translation) into our device, which will be done by the NIC interface. This can be done by inserting the "*iptables*" rule. This can be done as shown below:

```
iptables -t nat -A POSTROUTING -o eth0 -j MASQUERADE
```

We now need to perform our final testing. Plug your computer into the eth1 interface of the Pi device, and then plugin the onboard NIC into the modem.

The negotiation process will be done and after a short time, you will be in a position to access the Internet. However, it might fail to work. In this case, you have to use the IP that you assigned to the eth1 interface, which in my case is 192.168.160.1 and then ssh to the Pi. You should also run the command "*ifconfig*" so as to make sure that the eth0 interface has a public address. This is shown below:

```
sudo ifconfig -a
```

In my case, the command gives me the following output:

eth0   Link encap:Ethernet   HWaddr b8:27:eb:e8:4a:fe
      inet   addr:68.225.56.30 Bcast:68.225.52.255   Mask:255.255.255.0
      inet6 addr: fe80::ba27:ebff:fbe8:4ffe/64 Scope:Link
      UP BROADCAST RUNNING MULTICAST MTU:1500 Metric:1

RX packets:1851717 errors:0 dropped:0 overruns:0 frame:0

TX packets:680737 errors:0 dropped:0 overruns:0 carrier:0

collisions:0 txqueuelen:1000

RX bytes:1493496473 (1.3 GiB) TX bytes:131062180 (124.9 MiB)

eth1   Link encap:Ethernet HWaddr 40:3b:fc:00:74:b0

inet   addr:192.168.160.1 Bcast:192.168.160.255 Mask:255.255.255.0

inet6 addr: fe80::423c:fcff:fe00:74b0/64 Scope:Link

UP BROADCAST RUNNING MULTICAST MTU:1500 Metric:1

RX packets:674282 errors:0 dropped:0 overruns:0 frame:0

TX packets:1152146 errors:0 dropped:0 overruns:0 carrier:0

collisions:0 txqueuelen:1000

RX bytes:116080201 (110.7 MiB) TX bytes:1574122354 (1.3 GiB)

lo   Link encap:Local Loopback

inet addr:127.0.0.1 Mask:255.0.0.0

inet6 addr: ::1/128 Scope:Host

UP LOOPBACK RUNNING MTU:16436 Metric:1

RX packets:2 errors:0 dropped:0 overruns:0 frame:0

TX packets:2 errors:0 dropped:0 overruns:0 carrier:0

collisions:0 txqueuelen:0

RX bytes:152 (152.0 B) TX bytes:152 (152.0 B)

It is possible that your eth0 will still show a private address. This is an indication that it never renewed even after moving it to your modem. This problem can be solved by running the following command:

```
sudo ifdown eth0 && sudo ifup eth0
```

Run the *"ifconfig"* command to check the IP address and see if you are able to reach the Internet. You might be forced to reboot your modem, but avoid rebooting the Pi for some reasons.

If it fails to work at this point, begin from the first step, and ensure that no step is skipped. Note that the iptable rules which we inserted earlier are currently not persistent. This means that rebooting the pi will cause these to be overridden. To solve this problem, we need to save the rules, and then create a little script for restoring them when the network interfaces are started during the boot process.

The iptable rules can be saved as follows:

```
sudo iptables-save > /etc/iptables.up.rules
```

A script should then be created in the directory *"/etc/network/if-pre-up.d/"* and the following should be its content:

Begin by opening the file by use of the following command:

```
sudo nano /etc/network/if-pre-up.d/iptables
```

The following content should then be added to the file:

#!/bin/sh

#This script will restore iptables upon reboot

iptables-restore < /etc/iptables.up.rules

exit 0

For the script to run during the reboot, it must be made executable by use of the following command:

sudo chown root:root /etc/network/if-pre-up.d/iptables && sudo chmod +x /etc/network/if-pre-up.d/iptables && sudo chmod 755 /etc/network/if-pre-up.d/iptables

The command will change the ownership permissions of the file.

If you reboot at this time, you will find that the iptable rules have remained persistent.

For the sake of additional security, we should add some iptable rules as shown below:

sudo iptables -A INPUT -s 192.168.160.0/24 -i eth0 -j DROP

sudo iptables -A INPUT -s 10.0.0.0/8 -i eth0 -j DROP

sudo iptables -A INPUT -s 172.16.0.0/12 -i eth0 -j DROP

sudo iptables -A INPUT -s 224.0.0.0/4 -i eth0 -j DROP

sudo iptables -A INPUT -s 240.0.0.0/5 -i eth0 -j DROP

sudo iptables -A INPUT -s 127.0.0.0/8 -i eth0 -j DROP

sudo iptables -A INPUT -i eth0 -p tcp -m tcp --dport 22 -j DROP

sudo iptables -A INPUT -i eth0 -p icmp -m icmp --icmp-type 8 -j DROP

With the above rules, access from RFC 1918 subnets to your eth0 interface as well as ssh connections and ICMP packets. Once the changes have been made, they should be saved as follows:

```
sudo iptables-save > /etc/iptables.up.rules
```

To see the number of packets which your firewall has blocked, just execute the following command:

```
iptables -L -n -v
```

You should now be having a basic router which offers a low power consumption and some level of security. That is how the process can be done.

Chapter 3- Setting up GPIO (General Purpose Input Output)

The Raspberry Pi has a GPIO connector, and this can help you to attach external hardware to it. This is one of the greatest features offered by the device.

The GPIO connector offers a number of connections which are different. These include the following:

- True GPIO pins- which can be used for turning LEDs on and off.

- I2C interface pins- which can allow hardware modules to be connected with two pins.

- SPI interface with SPI devices- offers a different standard to that of I2C.

- Serial Rx and Tx pins- facilitates communication with serial peripherals.

In this chapter, we will explore how libraries can be added to the Raspberry Pi so that external electronics can be attached to it.

Adafruit Pi Code

This is just a collection of useful code which enables or helps the Pi users to easily attach electronics to their device. This is made up of a number of libraries in Python which can be supported in different modules. These include sensors, displays, and PMW controllers.

If you need to fetch the code, you must use the "*git*" software. On the Raspberry, this software must be installed unlike in Occidentalis in which it comes pre-installed. To perform the installation on the Raspberry, run the following commands on the LX terminal:

The icon for the LX terminal can be found on one's desktop, so just double-click on it in order to open it.

The command is as follows:

```
sudo apt-get update
```

With the above command, the respective package will be found and not only the package, but the latest version of it. Note that the command can be executed from any directory, and the effect will be the same. Note that the update process can take a long time if you have just executed the command for the first time in your Pi. When you see the prompt symbol displayed to you, just know that it is ready and the next command can be executed. The following should be the next command to be executed:

```
sudo apt-get install git
```

The above command is intended to install the *"git"* software. Once the installation process completes, just use the following commands so as to check the Adafruit Pi Python repository on your Pi:

The first command should be for cloning the repository, and it should be as follows:

```
git clone http://github.com/adafruit/Adafruit-Raspberry-Pi-Python-Code.git
```

You then have to change your working directory to the following directory:

```
cd Adafruit-Raspberry-Pi-Python-Code
```

You then have to list the contents of the directory as follows:

```
ls
```

In case a problem occurs during the above procedure, then an error message about the same will be printed out. In most cases, the kind of errors in this case might be caused by wrongly typing a certain command or a loss in the Internet connection.

Configuration of GPIO

Note that the pins of GPIO can be used both as digital inputs and digital outputs. When used as digital outputs, programs can be written for turning a particular pin either HIGH or LOW. When HIGH, it is at 3.3V and while low, it is at 0V. To drive an LED from any of the pins, then you need to connect a 1kΩ resistor in series with your GPIO pins. Note that with GPIO pins, only a small amount of power can be supported.

When the pin is used as a digital input, one can connect simple sensors and switches to the pin and then they will be able to check whether it is closed or open.

For the GPIO ports to be programmed in Python, a very important Python 2 library named *"Rpi.GPIO"* needs to be installed. This will help us with the management of the GPIO pins.

This should be installed in the same steps both in Occidentalis and in Raspberry. Some of the instructions used here will also update the software to the latest version. Begin by executing the following command:

```
sudo apt-get update
```

For the Rpi.GPIO to be installed, one must begin by installing the Python Development toolkit which is required by Rpi.GPIO.

Open the LX terminal, and then execute the following command:

```
sudo apt-get install python-dev
```

With the above command, the Python Development toolkit will be installed. Now you need to install the Rpi.GPIO itself, which can be done as follows:

```
sudo apt-get install python-rpi.gpio
```

When prompted to confirm the installation process, just type "*Y*" and the process will continue.

Configuration of I2C

This is a standard, and it was introduced as a way of enabling one chip to communicate to another. This means that the connection of the Raspberry can be done to several I2C capable modules and chips.

With the I2C bus, multiple devices can be connected to the Raspberry Pi and a unique address will be used for each. To change the address of any device, one has to change the setting of the jumper on the module. You need to be in a position to view the devices which are connected to your Raspberry so that you can determine whether everything is running correctly or not.

For this to be done, the i2-c utility has to be installed into the system by opening the terminal and then executing the following commands:

```
sudo apt-get install python-smbus
sudo apt-get install i2c-tools
```

Kernel support Installation

We now need to install the i2c support for the Linux kernel and ARM core. This can be done by running the following command:

```
sudo raspi-config
```

Once the above command has been executed, you have to follow the prompts which will be presented to you. Examples of these prompts are shown below:

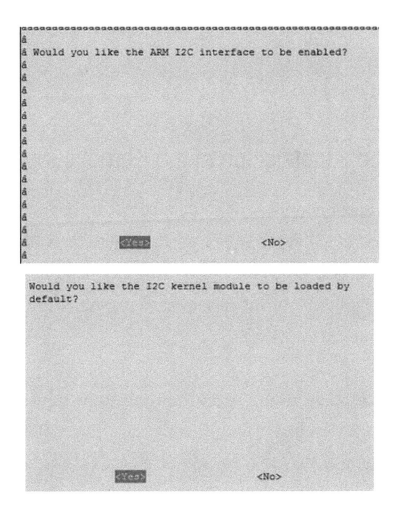

Once done, reboot your Pi so as to apply the changes you have made.

Manual Installation of the Kernel support

For Raspbian users, they must go through some further steps so as to set up their system ready for working. However, for those using Occidentalis, once the installation of I2c has succeeded, you are set and you can start working.

For Raspbian users, open the console or the ssh or the LXTerminal, and then run the following command:

```
sudo nano /etc/modules
```

The file will be opened. At the end of it, just add the following lines:

i2c-bcm2708

i2c-dev

This should be done as shown in the snapshot given below:

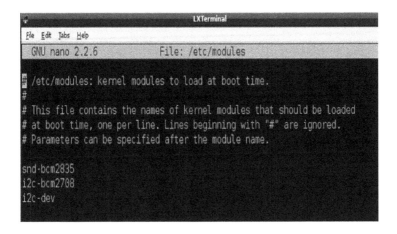

Once done, just save the file.

On your system, determine whether you have the file **_"/etc/modprobe.d/raspi-blacklist.conf."_** **If you fail to find it, then it is not there, but there is no problem. This depends on the distribution of Linux which you are using on your Pi. If you find the file, just open it, and then perform some editing on it by commenting out the following lines:**

blacklist spi-bcm2708

blacklist i2c-bcm2708

To comment the lines, you just have to add the pound (#) sign before the lines. An editor on the file should then be opened by running the following command:

```
sudo nano /etc/modprobe.d/raspi-blacklist.conf
```

The file will be opened. You then have to edit it so that it appears as shown below:

```
# blacklist spi and i2c by default (many users don't need them)

#blacklist spi-bcm2708
#blacklist i2c-bcm2708
```

Once edited, save the file and then exit. If the kernel of the Raspberry Pi which you are running is o version 3.18 and above, you have to update the file *"/boot/config.txt."* **Open the file by executing the following command:**

sudo nano /boot/config.txt

At the bottom of this file, just add the following lines:

dtparam=i2c1=on
dtparam=i2c_arm=on

Note the use of the number "1." Avoid confusing it with letter "L". The file should now be as follows:

```
hdmi_drive=2

# uncomment to increase signal to HDMI, if you have interference, blanking, or
# no display
#config_hdmi_boost=4

# uncomment for composite PAL
#sdtv_mode=2

#uncomment to overclock the arm. 700 MHz is the default.
#arm_freq=900

dtparam=i2c1=on
```

Once you done with the above, save and then reboot the system by running the following command:

sudo reboot

Testing I2C

We now need to view the devices which are connected to our Raspberry Pi. For those who are using the 512MB Raspberry Pi Model B, just open the terminal and then run the following command:

```
sudo i2cdetect -y 1
```

All the devices which are connected will be listed. For those who are using the 256MB Raspberry Pi Model B, then the command should be changed so that it is as shown below:

```
sudo i2cdetect -y 0
```

The devices will then be listed. Note that the differences in the devices is the ports.

Configuring SPI

We should start by removing any blacklist of the spi module. This can be done by running the following command:

```
sudo nano /etc/modprobe.d/raspi-blacklist.conf
```

This will open a text file. In it, look for the line **"blacklist spi-bcm2708." Comment it by adding the pound (#) sign before it. The file should then be as follows:**

```
# blacklist spi and i2

#blacklist spi-bcm2708
#blacklist i2c-bcm2708
blacklist snd-soc-pcm5
blacklist snd-soc-wm88
```

You can then save the changes and exit the file. Reboot the system by running the following command:

sudo reboot

The above command will apply the changes which you have made to the file. Once you login into the system, check for the devices with *"ls -l /dev/spidev*."* Two of these devices should be visible, and each will represent a SPI bus. This is shown below:

```
pi@pi2 ~ $ ls -l /dev/spidev*
crw-rw---T 1 root spi 153, 0 Jan  1  1970 /dev/spidev0.0
crw-rw---T 1 root spi 153, 1 Jan  1  1970 /dev/spidev0.1
```

Chapter 4- Sensing movement

The Raspberry Pi can be used for the purpose of sensing movement. In this case, a PIR motion detector is used. In this chapter, you will know how to use the Pi so as to detect movements and activate the door switch.

The following are the devices which are needed for the project to work:
PIR sensor, Magnetic Door Sensor, Half-size Breadboard, Jumper wire pack, and the Raspberry Pi. The following is the needed software for the program:

```
import time

import RPi.GPIO as io

io.setmode(io.BCM)

pir_pin = 18
```

```
door_pin = 23

io.setup(pir_pin, io.IN)            # activate
input

io.setup(door_pin,                      io.IN,
pull_up_down=io.PUD_UP)   # activate
input with PullUp

while True:

if io.input(pir_pin):

print("First Alarm!")

if io.input(door_pin):

print("Second Alarm!")

time.sleep(1)
```

With the above program, the pir_pin has been set to a plain old input. What the loop does is that it reads each of the inputs, and then it prints the appropriate message.

Configuration and testing

We now need to get everything working. The easiest way to get this working is establishing a connection to the Pi via SSH, and then using the following command to open the text editor:

```
nano switches.py
```

You then have to paste the following code to the file:

```
import time

import RPi.GPIO as io

io.setmode(io.BCM)

pir_pin = 18

door_pin = 23
```

```python
io.setup(pir_pin, io.IN)        # activate input
io.setup(door_pin, io.IN, pull_up_down=io.PUD_UP)  # activate input with PullUp
while True:
    if io.input(pir_pin):
        print("First Alarm!")
    if io.input(door_pin):
        print("Second Alarm!")
    time.sleep(1)
```

You can then save your file. We then need to start the actual demonstration.

Place the magnet and the switch close to each other. Take something, and then use it to cover the PIR sensor. You then have to run your program while logged in or as a super user. Use the following command:

```
sudo python switches.py
```

Once the command has been executed, some trace will be observed on the terminal once the cover has been taken away from the PIR sensor or once the magnet has been moved.

Chapter 5- MATLAB and Simulink for Raspberry

One can use MATLAB for communication with the Raspberry pi board and its peripheral devices by use of the MATLAB support package for the Raspberry pi.

The Raspberry pi boards can be programmed for running your algorithms by use of the Simulink support package for the Raspberry pi hardware. The support package will generate code from the Simulink model in just a click of a button, and then the Raspberry pi board will be run. Let us discuss this further.

Setting up MATLAB and Simulink package

Begin by opening the MATLAB, and then click on the drop down menu for Add-ons. This can be found at the top-right corner. This is shown in the figure given below:

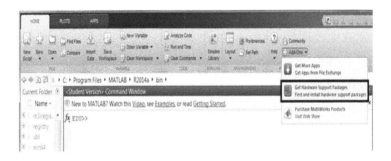

Starting the Support package Installer

We need to start the installer. This can be done by clicking on the *"Get Hardware Support Packages"* which can be found from the drop down. You then have to choose the source from which the support package will be installed. Just choose *"Install from Internet"* as shown in the figure given below:

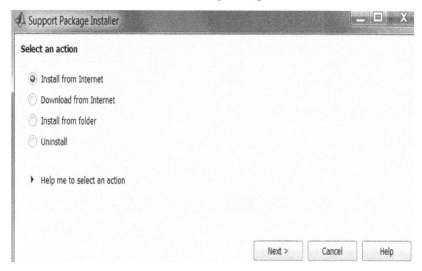

A list of support packages will be shown, so select *"Raspberry Pi."* All of the needed support packages will be installed at a go. This is shown in the figure given below:

MathWorks Account

You have to click on the button labeled *"Next"* so as to be able to log into this account. You will also be provided with the option of creating a new account in case you don't have one.

You should   accept the license, and then continue with the installation process by clicking on the *"Next"* buttons in the next screens which are to appear. This will install both the MATLAB and the Simulink Support packages for the Raspberry Pi.

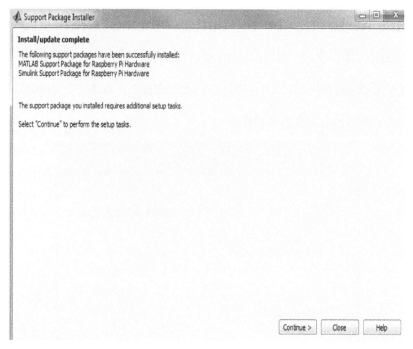

Once you reach the page for firmware update, select the appropriate model for your device. In my case, I have selected the following:

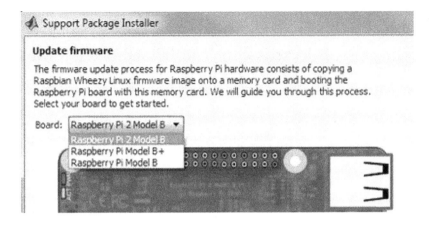

Click on the button labeled "*Next,*" and a screen for configure network will appear. Just choose the option which is shown in the figure given below:

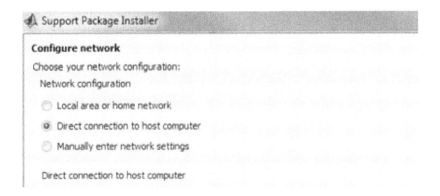

You will then be asked to select your drive. Note that all the MicroSD cards which MATLAB detects will be listed. It might happen that the MATLAB fails to detect a MicroSD card which has already been detected by the OS. In this case, you just have to close and then restart the MATLAB and all will be well. However, make sure that the MATLAB has been restarted while you are logged in as the administrator.

The next step should involve writing the firmware. Select the write option. This will erase all the contents which are contained in the memory card, and then the latest software which is needed by the support package will be written to the memory card.

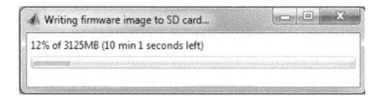

In the next steps, you just have to click on the *"Next"* button and the installation of the Simulink support package and MATLAB will complete.

How to use the MATLAB support package and the Raspberry Pi

We now have each of the required software already setup. We need to demonstrate how the MATLAB support and the Raspberry Pi can be used.

Open the MATLAB, and then run the following command:

```
>> mypi = raspi
```

When the above command is executed, a connection between the MATLAB and the Raspberry Pi will be established. A variable for the MATLAB will also be created, and this will be named "*mypi.*" This variable should now be visible on your workspace of the MATLAB. If an error occurred, then you see an error message instead of the variable. The variable will act as a representation of the connection established between the MATLAB and the Raspberry Pi, which is the physical object.

```
EDU>> mypi = raspi

mypi =
```

We now need to switch to the on-board LED which has been connected. This can be done by executing the following command:

```
>> writeLED(mypi,'led0',1)
```

With the above comamnd, a request has been send from the MATLAB to the connected Raspberry Pi board, and a value of 1 will be written to the on-board LED. The LED will also be switched ON by the above comamnd.

You might be interested in blinking the LED, which is a very nice feature. In this case, it must be switched ON and OFF most frequently. This can be achieved with the following code:

```
for j = 1:10
    writeLED(mypi,'ledo',1);
    pause(0.5);
    writeLED(mypi,'ledo',0);
    pause(0.5);
end
```

There are some other packages which are associated with the MATLAB support package for the Raspberry Pi. These functions can be used together with the Raspberry Pi object which we have created here, which is the *"mypi."* If you need to see some of the featured examples in your Raspberry Pi, just type the following command on the command line of the MATLAB:

raspi_examples

You need to be sure that the Raspberry Pi board is well connected to the computer which you are working with. To verify whether the connection was successful, just check on the lights which are on the ACT LED and the ones on the Ethernet port. If they are blinking, then know that the connection was successful and if not blinking, try to troubleshoot for problems.

How to use the Simulink support package and the Raspberry Pi

Begin by creating a Simulink model of your own. To do this, follow the steps given below:

1. Open the MATLAB. Click on *"New -> Simulink Model."* This can be found under the HOME tab.

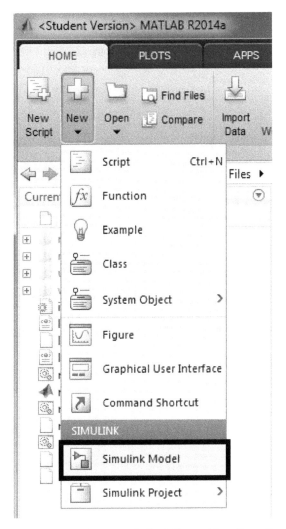

2. On your Simulink model, identify the "*Library Browser*" icon and then click on it. In the window for the Simulink Library Browser, navigate to the "*Sources*" tab.

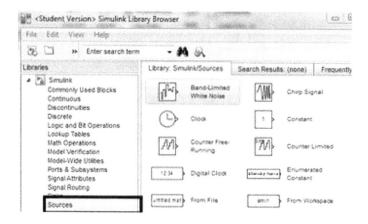

3. The *"Pulse Generator"* block should then be dragged from the sources library to the model. Its values should then be changed to the following:

Amplitude:

1

Period (number of samples):

2

Pulse width (number of samples):

1

Phase delay (number of samples):

0

Sample time:

1

☑ Interpret vector parameters as 1-D

OK	Cancel	Help	Apply

4. The LED block for the **Simulink Support Package for Raspberry Pi Hardware** should then be used in the Library browser, and the values changed as follows:

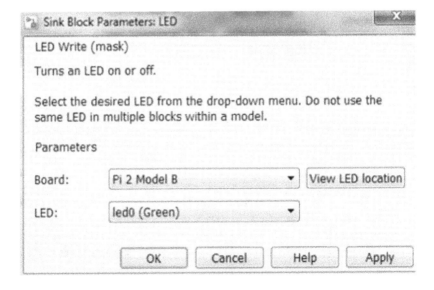

5. The block "*Data Type Conversion*" should the n be dragged and dropped from the tab labeled "*Signal Attributes*" under the Simulink Library.

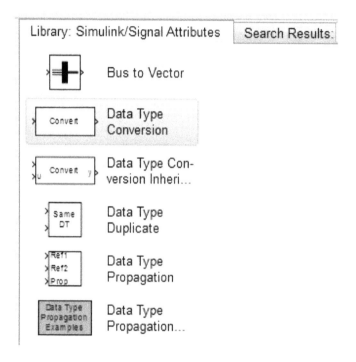

6. Identify and note the effect of moving the mouse pointer close to the arrow which is on the block. You will note that it will change to a plus sign. Once you observe this sign, just left click and then drag the mouse so as to make an

intended connection. After establishing the connection, the left click button can be released.

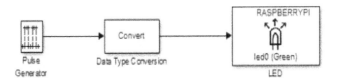

7. The model can then be saved. We now need to configure it. To do this, just navigate to **"Tools > Run on Target Hardware > Prepare To Run..."** This is shown below:

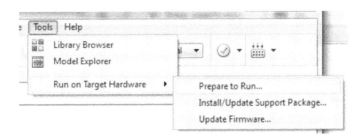

8. The page for *"Configuration Parameters"* will be opened. The parameter *"Target Hardware"* should be set to Raspberry Pi. The other settings should be left unchanged. This is shown in the figure given below:

9. You then have to click on the button labeled *"Deploy to Hardware"* in your Simulink Model. This can be found from the toolbar. The model will generate a particular code, and this can be deployed to the pi 2 device. Note that the on-board link should blink after every second.

Chapter 6- Temperature Sensing

This functionality can be achieved by the use of a temperature sensor named DS18B20 1-wire. It is supported in both Raspbian and Occidentalis. They come with a package which looks like a transistor and it has three pins. They are very accurate digital devices.

In this chapter, you will learn how to use this temperature sensor and the Raspberry Pi so as to take readings of temperature.

The following devices and parts will be needed so as to complete the project:

Raspberry Pi, DS18B20 Digital temperature sensor + extras, Half-sized breadboard, Jumper wire pack, and Pi Cobbler.

Hardware Layout

The layout of the devices in this case is very simple.

Connect the DS18B20 "1-wire" sensors in parallel. Note that all of the sensors should be sharing the same pins, and a single 4.7K resistor is needed. The resistor is needed as it should actor as a *"pullup"* for our data-line, and this will make sure that the data transfer is very stable. The curved edge of DS18B20 should be kept to the left. Putting it in the wrong side will make it overheat, and then it will break.

The DS18B20 "1-wire" might just look like a normal transistor. However, there are lots of processes taking place inside the device. It has output pins which are responsible for sending messages to the Raspberry in a digital form. The interface for the device is responsible for interpreting the messages. You can use SSH or the command line so as to experiment with the device.

On your command line, run the following command:

sudo nano /boot/config.txt

The above command will open a file in the text editor. What you do is scroll to the bottom of the file, and then add the following line of code to it:

dtoverlay=w1-gpio

You then have to reboot the system for the changes made to be applied. This can be done by running the following command:

sudo reboot

After the reboot is over and then you are logged in, type and run the following commands on the terminal:

sudo modprobe w1-gpio

sudo modprobe w1-therm

cd /sys/bus/w1/devices

ls

cd 28-xxxx (change this to match what serial number pops up)

cat w1_slave

The commands should be executed in the order given above, one after the other.

The interface can look somehow unreliable. However, it is responsible for telling us whether or not there are some temperatures which can be read. It can be compared to a file, so whatever is to be done is just read. After the first line is ended, you will notice a YES or NO response. If the response is YES, then you will observe the temperature at the end of the line, and this will be expressed in 1/1000 degrees Celsius.

In case more than one sensor has been connected to the system, then multiple 28-xxx files will be observed. Note that each of them will be identified by a unique serial number. This means that they can be plugged in one at a time. You can then look at the file which was created and then label the sensor.

Software

The following is the needed software, which is just a program written in Python. It will deal with messages which have failed and then after every second, the temperature will be reported in both degrees C and F. The program is as follows:

```
import time
```

```python
import os
import glob
os.system('modprobe w1-gpio')
os.system('modprobe w1-therm')
base_dir = '/sys/bus/w1/devices/'
device_folder = glob.glob(base_dir + '28*')[0]
device_file = device_folder + '/w1_slave'
def read_temp_raw():
file = open(device_file, 'r')
lines = file.readlines()
file.close()
return lines
def read_temp():
l = read_temp_raw()
while l [0].strip()[-3:] != 'YES':
```

```python
    time.sleep(0.2)

    l = read_temp_raw()

    equals_pos = l [1].find('t=')

    if equals_pos != -1:

        temp_string = l [1][equals_pos+2:]

        temp_c = float(temp_string) / 1000.0

        temp_f = temp_c * 9.0 / 5.0 + 32.0

        return temp_c, temp_f

while True:

    print(read_temp())

    time.sleep(1)
```

What the program does is that it begins by executing the *"modprobe"* commands. These commands are needed, as they usually launch the interface to be running. The file from which one can read the lines will also be found. However, when one is reading temperature files in Raspbian, there is the problem of frequent hangs which has been reported. In case you experience the same problem while doing this, identify the line with the function *"read_temp_raw,"* and then replace this with the following code:

```
def read_temp_raw():

cdata                                          =
subprocess.Popen(['cat',device_file],
stdout=subprocess.PIPE,
stderr=subprocess.PIPE)

out,err = cdata.communicate()

out_decode = out.decode('utf-8')

l = out_decode.split('\n')

return l
```

There are two methods which have been used for reading the temperature. The function "read_temp_raw" will fetch the two lines of messages from your interface. The function "read_temp" will then wrap up this and check for bad messages and then retry until there is a message having a "*YES*" at the end of its first line. Two values will form the return from the function. The first value will be the read temperature in degrees C while the second value will be the temperature in degrees F. To separate these two, use the code given below:

deg_c, deg_f = read_temp()

What the main loop of the program does is that it will loop throughout the program, read the value of temperature, and then print the value which has been read. It then sleeps for a second.

You then have to upload the program into your Raspberry Pi. This can be done by performing an SSH so as to connect to the Pi and then starting the editor window by executing the following command:

```
nano thermometer.py
```

You can then paste the code which we wrote previously into the file, and save the file. The code is shown below:

```python
def read_temp_raw():
    cdata = subprocess.Popen(['cat',device_file],
    stdout=subprocess.PIPE,
    stderr=subprocess.PIPE)
    out,err = cdata.communicate()
    out_decode = out.decode('utf-8')
    l = out_decode.split('\n')
    return l
```

Configuration and Testing

To run the program, you must have the privileges of the super user. To start the program, just run the following command on the terminal:

```
sudo python thermometer.py
```

A series of readings will then be observed once the above command has been executed. Warm the sensor a bit by just placing your finger on it.

You can also choose to add more sensors, in which case they should be connected in parallel. All the VCC for sensors should be connected, and the pins grounded. However, in the case of the resistor, it should not change, so use a single 4.7K resistor. Multiple *"/sys/bus/w1/devices/28-nnnnn"* directories will be observed, and each will have a unique serial number. The serial number will be used as the name of the directory.

Chapter 7- Email Notifier using LEDs

With this functionality, we will be in a position to know whenever we receive new email messages.

Remote SSH

A terminal on our Pi is needed. You need to know how to get a terminal on your Pi. You can then follow the steps given below:

1. Plug in your keyboard and HDMI monitor.
2. Use your console cable.

3. Use the SSH (Secure Shell) so as to login.

Note that in this project, GPIO pins are being used. This is why you need to choose to either work directly on the Pi or use the SSH so as to establish a connection to it. The first method is suitable when everything has already been set up, while the second method suits those who do not have input devices and an extra monitor around or near them, and still need to work from their laptop or desktop.

Preparation of Python

For our Python code to work effectively, there are a number of libraries which need to be installed.

Begin by executing the following command on either the SSH, keyboard, or monitor:

```
sudo apt-get install python-pip
```

When asked whether to continue, just type "*Y*" and then hit the Return key. The command will take some time before completing, so you need to be patient.

The next step should involve the installation of the IMAPClient Python Library, and this is responsible for enabling Python to talk to most of the e-mail services. Run the following command on the terminal so as to install this:

```
sudo pip install imapclient
```

The command will run in a verbose manner, and you will observe the following output on the terminal while it is being executed:

```
Downloading/unpacking imapclient
  Downloading IMAPClient-0.12.tar.gz (100Kb): 100Kb downloaded
  Running setup.py egg_info for package imapclient

Installing collected packages: imapclient
  Running setup.py install for imapclient

Successfully installed imapclient
Cleaning up...
pi@raspberrypi ~ $
```

With the current script, any version of the provider
can be supported as long as it supports access to
IMAP.

Some of you have also enabled the two-factor
authentication on their GMAIL account. If this is the
case on your system, then an application-specific
password need to be generated which will use IMAP.
If you are not sure of whether this factor is enabled
on your system, then you do not have to worry as this
is an indication that it is not enabled.

Wire LEDs

It is now time for us to wire up the LEDs. We can choose to use either the Pi Cobbler Plus or the Adafruit Pi Cobbler.

While connecting the GPIO cable, make sure that the white or red wire has been noted on the ribbon, which is the pin #1 of this cable. This side should be the one which is close to the SD card, and on your Pi, it should be labelled P1. The other side should be connected to the cobbler, and it only supports a one-way insertion due to the presence of a notch in the cable.

The cobbler should then be placed on the bread board and it should straddle the center line. The GND pin should then be connected to the blue power rail located on the side of the breadboard. Two resistors will also be needed.

The first resistor should be connected to the cobbler row which has been marked #18, and the other end of it should be connected to the row which has not been used by the cobbler.

The second resistor should then be connected to the cobbler which has been marked #23, and the other end of it should be connected to the empty row.

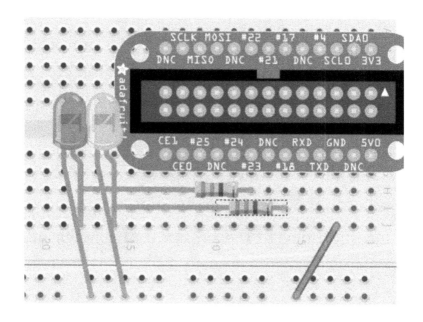

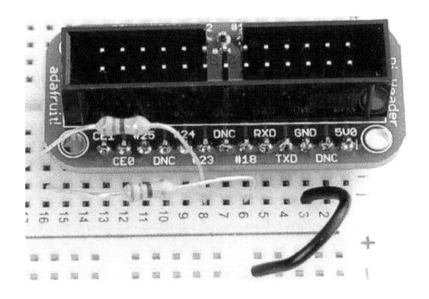

You can then grab the green LED and the red LED. Identify the long pins in the LEDs. They represent the positive (+) legs. The long (+) leg of the ribbon should be connected to the resistor which has been connected to #23 (GPIO #23). The long leg of the green LED should be connected to the resistor which has been connected to #18.

The short legs should then be plugged into the blue striped rail on the breadboard's side. This is shown in the figure given below:

Note that the images given in the above figures are for the original Pi Cobbler. If you are using the newer ones, then additional connections might be needed, and especially on the resistors and the LEDs. You are now done with the wiring part.

The Python Script

We then need to come up with the Python script which will be responsible for checking the Gmail IMAP email and then light up the green or red LEDs. The checking will be done using the IMAPClient.

You should create a new file and give it the name *"mailcheck.py."* This can be done by use of the following command:

nano mailcheck.py

From the extension given in the name of the file, it is very clear that the file will be a Python one. The following code should then be added to the file:

```python
#!/usr/bin/env python

import RPi.GPIO as GPIO

from imapclient import IMAPClient

import time

DEBUG = True

    HOSTNAME = 'imap.gmail.com'

    USERNAME = 'add your username'

    PASSWORD = 'add your password'

    MAILBOX = 'Inbox'

    NEWMAIL_OFFSET = 1    # provide the
    number of unread messages in your
    inbox

    MAIL_CHECK_FREQ = 60 # checking
    mail after every 60 seconds

    GPIO.setwarnings(False)

    GPIO.setmode(GPIO.BCM)
```

```python
GREEN_LED = 18

RED_LED = 23

GPIO.setup(GREEN_LED, GPIO.OUT)

GPIO.setup(RED_LED, GPIO.OUT)

def loop():

    serv = IMAPClient(HOSTNAME, use_uid=True, ssl=True)

    serv.login(USERNAME, PASSWORD)

    if DEBUG:

        print('Now logging in as ' + USERNAME)

    select_info = serv.select_folder(MAILBOX)

    print('%d messages in the INBOX' % select_info['EXISTS'])

    folder_status = server.folder_status(MAILBOX, 'UNSEEN')
```

```python
        nmails = int(folder_status['UNSEEN'])

        if DEBUG:

            print "There are", nmails, "new emails!"

    if nmails > NEWMAIL_OFFSET:

        GPIO.output(GREEN_LED, True)

        GPIO.output(RED_LED, False)

    else:

        GPIO.output(GREEN_LED, False)

        GPIO.output(RED_LED, True)

    time.sleep(MAIL_CHECK_FREQ)

if __name__ == '__main__':

    try:

        print 'You can quit by pressing Ctrl-C.'

        while True:

            loop()

    finally:
```

GPIO.cleanup()

There you have the code. Note that the username and the password that you provide should match the credentials for your Gmail account, otherwise errors will occur. An application-specific password also needs to be generated for this. For those of you who are using other email providers, you must check and know the Host to be used.

We now need to make our program executable. This can be done by executing the following command:

chmod +x mailcheck.py

The script can then be finally executed. This can be done by running the following command:

sudo ./checkmail.py

You can then try to send yourself some emails, and observe the green and red LEDs. These light up. It is also possible for you to stop the script at any time. This can be done by pressing Ctrl-C.

Chapter 8- Printing

It is possible for you to print something from the Pi in a printer which has been connected to the network which the Pi is also connected to. There are higher chances that this kind of printer is shared over the network. The printing to this kind of a printer from the Pi can be done as follows:

1. Open the LXTerminal and then run the following command:

   sudo apt-get install cups

2. When prompted to confirm, just type "y" and then hit the Return key.

3. On the same LXTerminal, type the following command:

sudo usermod -a -G lpadmin pi

You can then hit the Return key.

4. You can then open Midori. Navigate to its URL Bar, and then type the following URL:

http://127.0.0.1:631

5. The websites can be saved to favorites so as to reference them in the future.

6. Choose the "Administration" tab from your main screen.

7. Click on the *"Add Printer"* button.

8. Provide the username and the password for your Pi.

9. From the list of available printers, select yours, and then click on the *"Continue"* button.

10. You can then change the settings to satisfy your needs. In case you only have a single printer, just leave the settings as they are.

11. Click on the *"Continue"* button.

12. You can then select the model which is in close match to your printer.

13. Click on the button *"add printer."*

14. From the options provided, choose the best one to suit your printer.

15. Click on the button *"set default options."*

16. Click on the *"Printers"* tab. You can then print a test page.

If you open any applications which are capable of providing the printing service, then your printer will be visible here. However, while printing, avoid carrying out other tasks with the Pi as this can cause problems.

Conclusion

It can be concluded that the Raspberry Pi is a very useful device. Other than offering the basic services and functionalities which were discussed in the first part of this book, the device can be used to perform some other complex tasks. These have been discussed in this book. You need to begin by reading the first part of this book so as to equip yourself with the basic skills on how to use the Raspberry Pi. This will also make it easy for you to understand the content discussed in this book.

The Pi device can be used with MATLAB. This is a device which is highly used by technologists to perform some complex tasks. With the Raspberry Pi, one can also sense movement. You can then perform an action once the movement has been detected.

Temperature can also be measured and then recorded, and the recording will be done in both degrees C and degrees F. The device can also be used as a router. In this case, there are some configurations which will be needed. This book explores this.

The device also supports the use of the GPIO cable. This helps its users to attach external devices to it. Most people also find it difficult to realize whenever mails are send to them. However, with the Raspberry Pi, this problem can be solved. You just have to set up an email notifier which will notify you when an email is send to you. The LED lights on the device will light up when the mail has been received.

The above functionalities are an indication of how useful and functional the Raspberry Pi device is. Read the book, and then equip yourself with new skills. My hope is that the book has been helpful to you.